The Freelancer's Guide to Millwork Drafting
Using AutoCAD

By Negus Negesti

DEDICATION

To all my coworkers, friends, and family: Thank you for your unwavering support and encouragement, which motivated me to put my scattered thoughts and ideas on paper.

This book would not have been possible without the dedication and inspiration of those who worked with me. You are the driving force behind this guide, and I hold the upmost respect and gratitude for each of you.

In loving memory of Allen A. Sherrod

CONTENTS

ACKNOWLEDGMENTS

Sorrentino Mariani & Co
Island Architectural Woodworks
TS Woodworks & RAD Designs
USAM-DC
Apex Drafting & Partners

INTRODUCTION

Welcome to the world where creativity meets precision—
where every curve, edge, and joint is meticulously crafted to
bring beautiful designs to life. This book is your guide to
mastering AutoCAD for millwork drafting, an essential skill
for anyone involved in the intricate art of woodworking and
cabinetry design.

Millwork drafting is much more than drawing lines and
shapes on a screen; it's about translating ideas into detailed
plans that can be executed with accuracy and craftsmanship.
Whether you're an experienced drafter looking to refine
your skills or a beginner eager to learn the ropes, this book
will equip you with the knowledge and tools needed to
harness the full power of AutoCAD for millwork projects.

In the pages that follow, we'll explore the essential
techniques and best practices for using AutoCAD in millwork
drafting. From setting up your workspace and creating
precise drawings to understanding the nuances of
woodworking details, this book will guide you through the
entire process. You'll learn how to produce clear, accurate,
and professional-grade drawings that not only meet the
industry standards but also inspire the creation of stunning
millwork pieces.

Let's embark on this journey together, and by the end, you'll
have the confidence and expertise to turn your millwork
visions into reality with AutoCAD as your trusted tool.

1 Getting Started

THREE PILLARS OF SUCCESS

In the intricate world of millwork drafting, precision, efficiency, and accuracy are paramount. From custom cabinetry to intricate woodwork, every detail matters. To navigate this demanding landscape effectively, millwork drafters rely on three fundamental pillars: *drafting the right thing, drafting the thing right, and drafting fast*. Let's delve into each of these pillars and understand their significance in achieving excellence in millwork drafting.

PLANNING

Drafting the right thing is the foundation of successful millwork design. This pillar emphasizes the importance of understanding the client's vision, project requirements, and specifications before putting pen to paper or cursor to screen.

Key aspects of drafting the right thing include:

Client Collaboration

Effective communication and collaboration with clients are essential to grasp their unique needs, preferences, and design aesthetics. By actively listening to client feedback and incorporating their input into the drafting process, drafters can ensure that the final product aligns seamlessly with the client's expectations.

Comprehensive Planning

Thorough planning and meticulous attention to detail are crucial when drafting millwork designs. This involves conducting site measurements, assessing space constraints, and considering functional requirements to create designs that are not only aesthetically pleasing but also practical and functional.

Adherence to Building Codes and Standards

Compliance with building codes, regulations, and industry standards is non-negotiable in millwork drafting. Drafters must stay informed about relevant codes and standards governing materials, construction techniques, and safety requirements to ensure that their designs meet all the necessary criteria.

PROFICIENCY

Once the foundation is laid by drafting the right thing, the next pillar focuses on executing the design with precision and accuracy. *Drafting the thing right* involves meticulous attention to detail, technical proficiency, and adherence to industry best practices.

Key components of drafting the thing right include:

Technical Proficiency

Proficiency in drafting software and CAD (Computer-Aided Design) tools is essential for translating design concepts into detailed drawings and schematics accurately. As a drafter you must possess a deep understanding of drafting principles, geometric dimensioning and tolerancing (GD&T), and other technical aspects to ensure the accuracy and integrity of your work.

Material Knowledge

A comprehensive understanding of materials used in millwork, such as wood, veneers, laminates, and hardware, is essential for selecting appropriate materials and specifying their properties in the drafting process. Knowledge of material characteristics, durability, and finishing techniques will enable you to make informed decisions and create designs that meet both aesthetic and functional requirements.

Quality Control

Rigorous quality control measures are critical to identify and rectify any errors or inconsistencies in the drafting process. This includes reviewing drawings for accuracy, conducting thorough checks of dimensions and specifications, and collaborating with other team members, such as architects and engineers, to address any discrepancies or issues promptly.

PROMPT

While precision and accuracy are paramount, efficiency also plays a significant role in millwork drafting. Drafting fast involves optimizing workflows, leveraging technology, and adopting time-saving strategies to meet tight deadlines without compromising quality.

Key strategies for drafting fast include:

Workflow Optimization

Streamlining drafting workflows and processes can significantly improve efficiency and productivity. This may involve creating standardized templates, utilizing pre-existing design libraries, and implementing automation tools to reduce repetitive tasks and accelerate the drafting process.

Continuous Learning and Improvement

Investing in professional development and staying abreast of industry trends and advancements in drafting technology is essential for enhancing efficiency and proficiency. By continuously learning and honing your skills, you can leverage new tools and techniques to expedite the drafting process without sacrificing excellence.

Effective Time Management

Prioritizing tasks, setting realistic deadlines, and managing time effectively are crucial for meeting project timelines and delivering drafts promptly. As a drafter, I continue to work on allocating my time strategically to different phases of the drafting process, ensuring that each task receives adequate attention without causing delays.

Mastering millwork drafting requires a balanced approach that encompasses drafting the right thing, drafting the thing right, and drafting fast. By embracing these three pillars, millwork drafters can achieve excellence in their craft, deliver high-quality designs that meet client expectations, and navigate the complexities of the millwork industry with confidence and proficiency.

Tip:

CUSTOMIZE USER INTERFACE

The Customize User Interface (CUI) Editor is my go-to tool for tweaking various elements that kickstart commands in AutoCAD.

By customizing the interface, I can rearrange the tools I use frequently and introduce new ones to boost productivity. For instance, if I want a ribbon panel housing my most-used commands, I simply create a new Favorites ribbon panel in the CUI Editor and slot it onto the Home tab.

The CUI Editor splits into two parts:
1. **Customize Tab**: This tab is my playground for crafting and managing commands and elements that shape the interface. It's divided into three panes: Customizations In, Command List, and the Dynamic Display pane.

Customizations In Pane: Here, I navigate through loaded customization files to tweak various interface elements like ribbon tabs, panels, and the Quick Access toolbar. The tools at the top help me load partial customization files, save changes, and manage how I view the loaded files.

The tree view within this pane aids in creating and managing UI elements. Once an element is set up, I drag commands from the Command List pane to add them. I can also reorder commands on elements like ribbon panels or toolbars by dragging them up and down the tree view.

2. **Transfer Tab**: This tab lets me create and save a CUIx file and transfer UI elements between CUIx files.

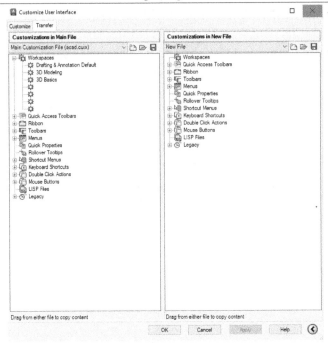

Before diving into customizing ribbon tabs, panels, or Quick Access toolbars, I always make sure to get comfortable with the CUI Editor. Opening it up with the CUI command gets me started, and from there, I explore the Customize tab to shape my AutoCAD experience just the way I like it.

BRIDGING THE GAP: DRAFTING TO ENGINEERING

As a seasoned millwork drafter, I've had the privilege of working closely with engineering teams on countless projects. Over the years, I've come to appreciate the importance of collaboration and communication in ensuring that millwork designs seamlessly integrate with the broader architectural and structural framework of a building or space. In this chapter, I'll share insights into the process of drafting millwork that works harmoniously with the broader spectrum of engineering teams.

Understanding the Big Picture

The first step in drafting millwork that complements the engineering team's efforts is to understand the broader context of the project. This involves familiarizing oneself with the architectural plans, structural drawings, and other relevant documents to gain a comprehensive understanding of the building's design intent and structural requirements. By understanding the big picture, millwork drafters can ensure that their designs align with the overall vision of the project and combine seamlessly with the building's structural framework.

Collaborative Communication

Effective communication is key to successful collaboration between millwork drafters and engineering teams. This involves regular meetings, discussions, and exchanges of information to ensure that everyone is on the same page regarding project requirements, constraints, and timelines. By fostering open lines of communication, millwork drafters can address any potential conflicts or discrepancies early in the design process, minimizing the need for costly revisions later on.

Integration of Design and Functionality

One of the challenges of drafting millwork in collaboration with engineering is balancing design aesthetics with functional requirements. As a millwork drafter, you must not only create visually appealing designs but also ensure that they meet the structural and performance criteria set forth by the engineering team. This may involve incorporating structural reinforcements, specifying appropriate materials, and accommodating mechanical, electrical, and plumbing (MEP) requirements within the millwork design.

Embracing Innovation and Technology

In today's digital age, drafting millwork for seamless integration with the engineering team often involves leveraging advanced technologies and software tools. Building Information Modeling (BIM) software, in particular, has revolutionized the way millwork drafters collaborate with engineering teams by enabling the creation of detailed, three-dimensional models that incorporate architectural, structural, and MEP elements. By embracing innovation and technology, millwork drafters can modernize the design process, improve accuracy, and enhance collaboration with engineering teams.

Drafting millwork that seamlessly mixes with the engineering team is a collaborative effort that requires effective communication, understanding of project requirements, and integration of design and functionality. By fostering open lines of communication, embracing innovation and technology, and committing to continuous learning and improvement, millwork drafters can ensure that their designs not only meet the aesthetic vision of the project but also align with the structural and performance criteria set forth by the engineering team.

DECODING ARCHITECTURAL DRAWINGS

As a millwork professional tasked with creating shop drawings, the ability to read and interpret architectural drawings is a critical skill. Architectural drawings serve as the blueprint for a construction project, providing detailed information about dimensions, materials, and construction methods. In this chapter, we'll explore how to effectively read and interpret architectural drawings to create accurate and comprehensive shop drawings.

Understanding Plan Types

Architectural drawings come in various types, each serving a specific purpose in the construction process. The most common types of architectural drawings include floor plans, elevations, sections, and details.

Floor Plans: Floor plans provide a bird's-eye view of a building's layout, showing the arrangement of rooms, walls, doors, and windows.

Reflected Ceiling Plan (RCP): is a type of architectural drawing that provides a detailed overhead view of the ceiling layout within a building or space.
I learned a valuable lesson early in my career to be cognizant that when drafting using the RCP, the public's view will be opposite of what is shown in the RCP. Drafting tip: Imagine yourself looking up at the ceiling to get a true understanding of the scope of work.

Elevations: Elevations depict the exterior or interior faces of a building, showing the height and width of architectural elements such as walls, windows, and doors.

Sections: Sections are vertical slices through a building and millwork components, showing the relationship between interior spaces and structural elements such as walls, floors, and ceilings. At times, a horizontal slice may be required for more clarity.

Details: Details provide close-up views of specific construction elements, such as joints, connections, and finishes.

There are times you may find contradictions in the architectural drawings. My rule of thumb when dealing with opposing interpretations:

- Details override Sections.
- Sections override Elevations.
- Elevations override Plans.

Always consult the design team before deciding which design intent you should be following.

Understanding Scale and Dimensions

Architectural drawings are typically drawn to scale, meaning that the size of objects and spaces is represented proportionally to their actual size. Understanding scales is crucial for accurately interpreting dimensions and measurements on architectural drawings. Common scales used in architectural drawings include 1/4" = 1'-0" (quarter-inch scale) and 1/2" = 1'-0" (half-inch scale).

When reading architectural drawings, it's important to pay attention to dimensions, annotations, and symbols that indicate the size, location, and orientation of architectural elements. This information is essential for creating shop drawings that accurately reflect the intended design and dimensions of millwork components.

Identifying Key Information

In addition to dimensions and scale, architectural drawings contain a wealth of information that is pertinent to creating shop drawings. This includes:

Material Specifications: Architectural drawings often specify the materials to be used for various construction elements, such as wood species, finishes, and hardware.

Construction Details: Details on architectural drawings provide important information about how various components are assembled, joined, and finished. Understanding these details is crucial for creating shop drawings that adhere to the design intent and construction standards.

Callouts and Annotations: Callouts and annotations on architectural drawings highlight important features, notes, and instructions that may impact the design and construction of millwork components. Paying close attention to these annotations ensures that shop drawings accurately reflect the architect's intent.

Collaboration with Design Team

Interpreting architectural drawings for shop drawings is not a solitary endeavor—it requires collaboration and communication with the design team, including architects, designers, project managers, GCs, and engineers. Building a collaborative relationship with the design team ensures that any questions or uncertainties about the drawings can be addressed promptly and accurately, resulting in shop drawings that meet the design aesthetic and project requirements.

The ability to read and interpret architectural drawings is essential for creating accurate and comprehensive shop drawings in the millwork industry. By understanding plan types, scale and dimensions, identifying key information, and collaborating effectively with the designers, millwork professionals can ensure that their shop drawings are accurately reflected and meet the specifications of the project. Through careful interpretation and attention to detail, shop drawings play a critical role in translating architectural vision into tangible, functional, and beautifully crafted millwork art.

SETTING UP YOUR ENVIRONMENT

As someone who has navigated the intricate world of AutoCAD for years, I understand the importance of having a well-organized and standardized workspace. Whether you're a seasoned CAD professional or just starting your journey with AutoCAD, preparing your environment to company standards can significantly improve efficiency, consistency, and collaboration within your team. In this chapter, I'll share my insights and tips on how to set up your AutoCAD environment to any company standards.

Understand Company Standards

The first step in preparing your AutoCAD environment to company standards is to familiarize yourself with the company's specific CAD standards and protocols. These standards may include layer naming conventions, linetypes, text styles, dimension styles, and other drawing settings that are unique to the organization you are working with. Take the time to review the company's CAD standards documentation thoroughly and ensure that you understand their requirements and expectations.

Customize Your Workspace

Once you've familiarized yourself with the company's CAD standards, it's time to customize your AutoCAD workspace to align with those standards. This may involve creating custom templates, tool palettes, and menu configurations that reflect the company's preferred settings and workflows. Consider organizing your tool palettes and menus logically, grouping related tools and commands together for easy access.

Set Up Layers and Linetypes

Layers play a crucial role in organizing and managing the elements of your AutoCAD drawings. Follow your company's layer naming conventions and create a set of standard layers that align with your organization's requirements.

Define Text and Dimension Styles

Consistent text and dimension styles are essential for maintaining clarity and readability in your AutoCAD drawings. Create custom text and dimension styles that adhere to your company's standards, including font type, size, color, and other formatting options. Use these standardized styles consistently throughout your drawings to ensure uniformity and professionalism.

Implement Plotting and Publishing Standards

Ensure that your plotting and publishing settings are configured to meet your company's requirements for outputting drawings. Set up plot styles, paper sizes, plot scales, and other plotting parameters according to your organization's standards. Test your plotting settings to verify that they produce the desired results and meet your company's quality control guidelines.

Most millwork manufacturers will have a custom plot style (.ctb) readily available at your request.

Document Your Customizations

Once you've customized your AutoCAD environment to company standards, document your settings and configurations for future reference. Create a reference guide or documentation manual that outlines each company's CAD standards when working with multiple clients and provides instructions on how to set up AutoCAD to adhere to those standards. This documentation will be invaluable in case of system failure of sorts or sharing with other team members and ensuring consistency across projects.

By customizing your workspace, setting up layers and linetypes, defining text and dimension styles, implementing plotting and publishing standards, and documenting your customizations, you can ensure that your AutoCAD environment aligns with your organization's requirements and facilitates seamless collaboration within your team.

With a standardized AutoCAD environment, you'll be better equipped to tackle projects confidently and produce high-quality drawings that meet your company's standards and exceed client expectations.

Tip:

CREATING WORKSPACES

Workspaces are sets of menus, toolbars, palettes, and ribbon control panels that you can group and organize to create a custom, task-oriented drawing environment. I strongly recommend setting up your workspaces to be client-oriented if you work with multiple clients. By doing this, only the menus, toolbars, and palettes relevant to a client are displayed. Additionally, a workspace may automatically display the ribbon, a special palette with task-specific control panels.

When making changes to your drawing display, such as moving, hiding, or displaying a toolbar or a tool palette group, and you want to preserve the display settings for future use, you can save the current settings to a workspace.

Switch Workspaces

You can switch to another workspace whenever you need to work on a different project for a different client by using the Workspace Switching button on the status bar at the bottom-right of the application window.

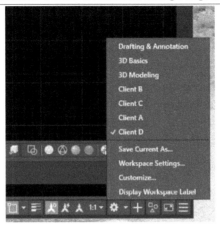

Create or Change a Workspace

You can create your own workspaces and modify the default ones. To create or change a workspace, I use either of the following methods:

1. Display, hide, and rearrange my toolbars and windows, modify my ribbon settings, and then save the current workspace from the Workspace Switching button in the status bar, the Workspaces toolbar, or the Window menu. I can also use the WORKSPACE command.
2. For more extensive changes, I open the Customize User Interface dialog box to set up the workspace environment.

You can control the display order of your saved workspace and other options in the Workspace Settings dialog box.

Note: When you make changes to the drawing display, the changes are stored in your profile and are displayed the next time you launch the program, regardless of your workspace settings. The profile changes are not automatically saved to a workspace unless you select the Automatically Save Workspace Changes option in the Workspace Settings dialog box. To preserve profile settings in a workspace, you click Save Current As from the shortcut menu of the Workspace Switching icon on the status bar.

2 Standards

AWI STANDARDS

In the intricate world of millwork, where craftsmanship meets precision, adherence to standards plays a pivotal role in ensuring quality, consistency, and customer satisfaction. Among the most renowned and respected standards in the industry are those set forth by the Architectural Woodwork Institute (AWI). In this chapter, we'll explore the significance of AWI standards and their impact on the millwork industry.

Setting the Standard

Established in 1953, the Architectural Woodwork Institute is a nonprofit organization dedicated to advancing excellence in the woodworking industry. AWI's mission is to promote the highest standards of craftsmanship, professionalism, and integrity among its members, which include manufacturers, suppliers, and installers of architectural woodwork.
At the heart of AWI's efforts are its comprehensive standards, known as the Architectural Woodwork Standards (AWS). These standards serve as a benchmark for quality and performance in the millwork industry, providing detailed guidelines for the fabrication, installation, and finishing of architectural woodwork. By adhering to AWS, millwork professionals can ensure that their work meets the highest standards of quality and craftsmanship.

THE SIGNIFICANCE OF AWI STANDARDS

The importance of AWI standards in the millwork industry cannot be overstated. Here are some key reasons why adherence to these standards is essential:

Quality Assurance

AWI standards define the minimum acceptable quality for architectural woodwork, covering everything from materials and construction methods to finishing techniques and installation procedures. By following these standards, millwork professionals can maintain consistent quality across all aspects of their work, ensuring that every project meets or exceeds client expectations.

Consistency

Consistency is crucial in the millwork industry, where even minor variations in dimensions, finishes, or detailing can detract from the overall aesthetic and functionality of a space. AWI standards provide clear and precise guidelines for achieving uniformity and consistency in architectural woodwork, helping to ensure that every component fits seamlessly into its intended environment.

Customer Confidence

When clients see that a millwork project has been completed in accordance with AWI standards, they can have confidence in its quality, durability, and longevity. AWI certification serves as a mark of excellence, distinguishing millwork professionals who uphold the highest standards of craftsmanship and professionalism.

Industry Reputation

Adherence to AWI standards not only benefits individual millwork professionals but also elevates the reputation of the industry as a whole. By promoting a culture of excellence and accountability, AWI standards help to safeguard the integrity and reputation of the millwork industry, positioning it as a trusted partner in the construction and design process.

Implementing AWI Standards

Implementing AWI standards requires a commitment to excellence and a willingness to invest in training, resources, and infrastructure. Millwork professionals must familiarize themselves with the requirements outlined in the AWS and ensure that their practices and processes align with these standards. This may involve ongoing training and education, as well as regular audits and inspections to monitor compliance.

Additionally, collaboration and communication are key to successful implementation of AWI standards. Millwork professionals must collaborate closely with architects, designers, contractors, and other stakeholders to ensure that project requirements are clearly understood and executed according to AWI standards. By fostering a culture of collaboration and transparency, millwork professionals can deliver exceptional results that meet the highest standards of quality and craftsmanship.

AWI standards play a vital role in upholding excellence in the millwork industry, offering clear guidelines for quality, consistency, and professionalism, enabling millwork professionals to achieve exceptional results that fulfill or surpass client imaginations. As the industry continues to evolve, adherence to AWI standards will remain essential for maintaining the integrity and reputation of the millwork profession.

THE AMERICANS WITH DISABILITIES ACT

In the dynamic world of millwork, where design meets functionality, adherence to accessibility standards is paramount to creating spaces that are inclusive and accommodating to all individuals. Among the most crucial sets of regulations governing accessibility is the Americans with Disabilities Act (ADA). In this chapter, we'll explore the significance of ADA standards in the millwork industry and their impact on design, construction, and user experience.

Understanding the ADA Standards

Enacted in 1990, the Americans with Disabilities Act is a landmark civil rights law in the U.S. that prohibits discrimination against individuals with disabilities in all areas of public life, including employment, transportation, and public accommodations. Title III of the ADA specifically addresses accessibility requirements for public spaces, including commercial buildings, retail establishments, and places of public accommodation.

The ADA Standards for Accessible Design establish specific guidelines and requirements for ensuring accessibility in the built environment. These standards cover a wide range of architectural elements, including doors, ramps, signage, and, importantly for the millwork industry, cabinetry, counters, and other built-in furniture. By adhering to ADA standards, millwork professionals can create spaces that are accessible, safe, and welcoming to individuals of all abilities.

Significance of ADA Standards in Millwork

The importance of ADA standards in the millwork industry cannot be overstated. Here are some key reasons why adherence to these standards is essential:

Inclusivity

ADA standards ensure that spaces are designed to accommodate individuals with a wide range of disabilities, including mobility impairments, visual impairments, and hearing impairments. By incorporating accessible design features into millwork components such as cabinetry, counters, and shelving, millwork professionals can create environments that are welcoming and inclusive to all individuals, regardless of their abilities.

Compliance

Adherence to ADA standards is not only a legal requirement but also a moral imperative. Failure to comply with ADA regulations can result in costly fines, legal liabilities, and reputational damage. By familiarizing themselves with ADA requirements and integrating accessible design principles into their work, millwork drafters can ensure compliance with the law and avoid potential legal consequences.

User Experience

Accessibility is not just a legal requirement, it's also essential for providing positive user experience. Millwork components that are designed with accessibility in mind are easier to use, safer, and more comfortable for individuals with disabilities. By incorporating features such as adjustable-height counters, accessible storage solutions, and tactile signage, millwork professionals can enhance the usability and functionality of spaces for all users.

Universal Design

In addition to meeting the specific requirements of the ADA, millwork professionals can also embrace the principles of universal design, which aim to create environments that are usable by people of all ages, abilities, and backgrounds. Universal design goes beyond minimum accessibility requirements to create spaces that are intuitive, flexible, and accommodating to diverse needs and preferences.

Implementing ADA Standards in Millwork

Implementing ADA standards in millwork projects requires careful planning, attention to detail, and collaboration with designers, architects, and other stakeholders. Millwork professionals must familiarize themselves with the specific requirements outlined in the ADA Standards for Accessible Design and ensure that their work complies with these regulations.

This may involve incorporating features such as accessible countertop heights, clear floor space for wheelchair maneuverability, and tactile indicators for individuals with visual impairments. Additionally, millwork professionals should stay abreast of updates and revisions to ADA standards to ensure that their work remains compliant with current regulations.

ADA standards play a vital role in promoting accessibility and inclusivity in the millwork industry. By adhering to these standards, drafters can create spaces that are welcoming, functional, and safe for individuals of all abilities. As the industry continues to evolve, compliance with ADA standards will remain essential for creating environments that are accessible and accommodating to everyone.

THE IMPORTANCE OF COMPANY STANDARDS

As a drafter, I cannot overemphasize the importance of adhering to millwork company standards in the architectural and construction industries. Millwork is vital in bringing a design to life, encompassing intricate wood paneling, cabinetry, custom doors, and molding. Following these standards ensures the seamless integration of these elements into your designs.

Consistency and Quality Assurance

Adhering to millwork company standards allows me to maintain a consistent quality level across all projects. These standards often include specifications for materials, dimensions, finishes, and construction methods. By following these guidelines, I ensure that every piece of millwork meets the company's quality criteria, which are crucial for maintaining the company's reputation and delivering a product that meets client expectations.

Streamlined Production Process

Following established standards also enables me to create designs optimized for the company's production capabilities. This means using standard dimensions, materials, and construction techniques that the millwork company can handle effectively and efficiently. This alignment between design and production reduces errors, minimizes waste, and speeds up the manufacturing process, ultimately leading to cost savings and faster project completion times.

Compatibility and Integration

When designing millwork components, it is essential for drafters to ensure they seamlessly integrate with other building elements such as walls, floors, and ceilings. By adhering to millwork company standards, we ensure our designs are compatible with these elements, reducing the risk of installation issues. This is particularly important for custom projects where precision and fit are critical. Following the standards helps avoid costly modifications and delays during installation.

This also includes visualizing how certain millwork components can be maneuvered throughout the building for installation purposes. For example, knowing the elevator's inner dimensions that will be used to transport will help determine if there are any size restrictions to take into consideration when designing cabinetry, wall panels, and other millwork products.

Compliance with Regulations and Codes

Millwork standards often incorporate industry regulations and building codes, such as AWI standards and ADA (Americans with Disabilities Act) requirements. By adhering to these standards, I ensure my designs comply with safety and accessibility requirements. This compliance is essential for obtaining necessary permits and avoiding legal issues, providing peace of mind to clients, knowing their project meets all relevant regulations.

Effective Communication and Collaboration

When all team members and coworkers follow the same standards, communication and collaboration become more efficient. Adhering to these standards ensures that my designs are easily understood and interpreted, reducing the risk of miscommunication. This shared understanding fosters a collaborative environment where everyone is working towards the same goals and expectations.

Customization Within Frameworks

While standards provide a framework for consistency, they do not stifle creativity. There is ample space to create unique and customized designs within these boundaries. This balance between standardization and customization allows millwork companies to offer bespoke solutions that meet individual client needs while maintaining control over quality and production processes.

Enhancing Client Satisfaction

Clients expect high craftsmanship and attention to detail in millwork projects. By following established standards, we contribute to delivering a product that meets or goes beyond client expectations. Consistency in quality, timely delivery, and seamless installation all contribute to higher levels of client satisfaction and the potential for repeat business and referrals.

In my role as a drafter, adherence to company standards is not merely a formality but a necessity for ensuring quality, efficiency, and client satisfaction. These standards provide a clear roadmap for creating designs that are aesthetically pleasing, functional, compliant, and manufacturable. By following these guidelines, we play a crucial role in upholding the integrity and reputation of the millwork company, ultimately contributing to the success of each project and the satisfaction of every client.

Tip:

MANAGING LAYERS

Layer filters are customizable criteria that allow you to sort and display only the layers you need at any given time. Instead of scrolling through a long list of layers, you can create filters to quickly access relevant layers based on their properties, such as name, color, linetype, or even custom attributes. This can be particularly useful when working on complex drawings where layers are grouped by different disciplines, phases, or other organizational schemes.

Types of Layer Filters:

- Property Filters
- Group Filters

Here's how you can create and use layer filters:
1. Accessing the Layer Properties Manager: Open the Layer Properties Manager by typing `LAYER` into the command line or clicking on the Layer Properties icon in the ribbon. This is where you can manage all aspects of layers, including creating filters. (*See IMG 1*)

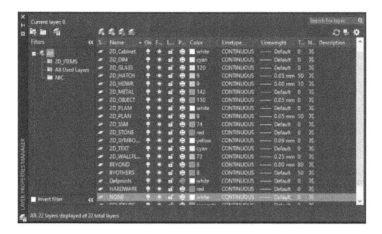

IMG1

2. Creating a Property Filter:

In the Layer Properties Manager (*See IMG2*), click on the New Property Filter button.

A dialog box will appear, prompting you to name your filter and define the criteria.

For example, you could create a filter named "Red Layers" and set the color criterion to "Red."

Once the filter is created, only layers matching these criteria will be displayed when the filter is active.

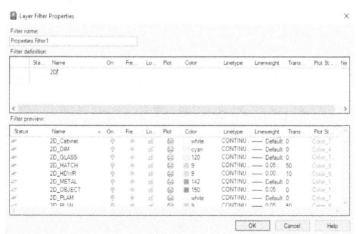

IMG2

3. **Creating a Group Filter**:

To create a group filter, click on the New Group Filter button in the Layer Properties Manager.

Name your filter, and then manually drag and drop the desired layers into the group.

Group filters are particularly useful for organizing layers that you frequently need to access together, regardless of their properties. (*See IMG3*)

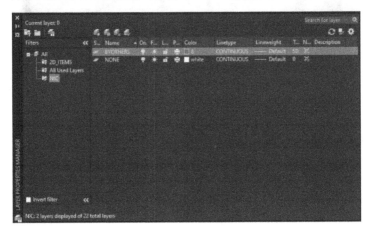

IMG3

4. **Applying Filters**:

Once created, you can activate a filter by selecting it from the Layer Properties Manager. This will display only the layers that meet the filter's criteria, hiding the rest from view.

This makes it easier to focus on specific parts of your drawing without the distraction of unrelated layers. (*See IMG4*)

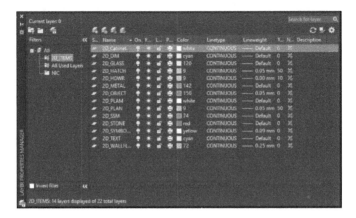

IMG4

Practices for Using Layer Filters

To maximize the efficiency of layer filters, consider these best practices:

Name Filters Clearly: Use descriptive names for your filters so you can easily identify their purpose. For example, instead of naming a filter "Filter1," use "3D" or "Not In Scope."

Combine Filters: Don't be afraid to combine different filters for greater control. For example, you might have a property filter for layers related to electrical work and a group filter for layers used in a specific drawing phase. Switching between these filters can help you manage large projects more effectively.

Regularly Update Filters: If you frequently add new layers, ensure that your property filters are still relevant. Periodically review and update your filters to keep them aligned with your project's evolving needs.

Use Filters to Improve Performance: In large, complex drawings, using filters to hide unnecessary layers can improve performance, as AutoCAD doesn't need to process and display as many elements.

By creating and using both property and group filters, you can quickly access the layers you need, reduce clutter, and focus on the task at hand.

3 Millwork Construction

MILLWORK CONSTRUCTION METHODS

Welcome to the fascinating world of millwork construction methods, where craftsmanship meets innovation to create architectural masterpieces. As someone deeply passionate about the art of millwork, I am excited to take you on a journey through the various techniques and approaches that define our craft.

In this chapter, we will delve into the diverse range of millwork construction methods, exploring their unique characteristics, applications, and intricacies. From traditional joinery techniques passed down through generations to cutting-edge manufacturing processes driven by technology, we will uncover the rich tapestry of methods that shape the landscape of "art-ectural" millwork.

Traditional Joinery

Let us begin our exploration with the timeless art of traditional joinery. Rooted in centuries of craftsmanship, traditional joinery techniques such as dovetailing, mortise and tenon, and tongue and groove, exemplify the marriage of skill and precision. We will delve into the intricacies of each technique, exploring their strengths, limitations, and applications in modern millwork projects.

Modern CNC Machining

Next, we turn our attention to the realm of modern CNC machining, where precision meets efficiency to revolutionize millwork construction. With the advent of computer-aided design (CAD) and computer numerical control (CNC) technology, millworkers can now achieve unparalleled levels of accuracy and complexity in their creations. We will explore the capabilities of CNC machining, from intricate carving and shaping to precise cutting and drilling, and its role in shaping the future of millwork construction.

Prefabrication and Modular Construction

Prefabrication and modular construction methods have emerged as innovative solutions to streamline the millwork manufacturing process and enhance project efficiency. By prefabricating millwork components off-site in controlled environments, millworkers can reduce waste, improve quality control, and accelerate project timelines. We will examine the benefits and challenges of prefabrication and modular construction, and their growing significance in modern construction practices.

Hybrid Approaches

In today's dynamic landscape of millwork construction, hybrid approaches that combine traditional craftsmanship with modern technology are increasingly prevalent. Whether it's integrating handcrafted elements with CNC-machined components or leveraging prefabrication techniques alongside on-site assembly, hybrid approaches offer a flexible and adaptive framework for meeting the diverse needs of millwork projects. We will explore examples of hybrid approaches and their potential to push the boundaries of innovation in millwork construction.

As we journey through the diverse array of millwork construction methods, I invite you to embark on a voyage of discovery and inspiration. Whether you're a seasoned professional or an aspiring enthusiast, there is always something new to learn and explore in the ever-evolving world of architectural millwork. Together, let us celebrate the artistry, craftsmanship, and ingenuity that define our beloved craft.

TRADITIONAL MILLWORK JOINERY

In the world of architectural millwork, traditional joinery techniques stand as a testament to the time-honored craft of woodworking. From intricate dovetails to sturdy mortise and tenon joints, these methods have been passed down through generations, embodying the essence of craftsmanship and precision. Let us begin exploring some of the most iconic examples of traditional millwork joinery and uncover the beauty and ingenuity behind each technique.

Dovetail Joinery

Dovetail joints are perhaps one of the most recognizable and revered examples of traditional millwork joinery. Characterized by interlocking trapezoidal-shaped pins and tails, dovetail joints are renowned for their strength, durability, and aesthetic appeal. Whether used in drawer construction or cabinet making, dovetail joints showcase the skill and mastery of the craftsman, creating seamless and visually striking connections that stand the test of time.

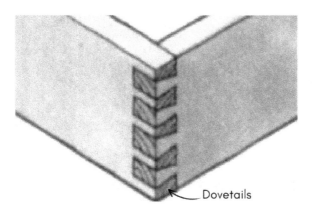

Dovetails

Mortise and Tenon Joints

Mortise and tenon joints represent another cornerstone of traditional millwork joinery, dating back thousands of years to ancient civilizations such as the Egyptians and the Greeks. This time-tested method involves inserting a protruding tenon into a corresponding mortise, creating a strong and reliable connection that is ideal for structural applications such as framing, cabinetry, and furniture construction. Mortise and tenon joints come in various forms, including through mortise and tenon, blind mortise and tenon, and haunched mortise and tenon, each tailored to suit specific design requirements and aesthetic preferences.

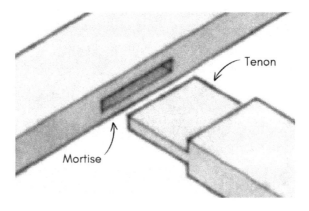

Tongue and Groove Joints

Tongue and groove joints are commonly used in millwork applications where seamless paneling or flooring is desired. This simple yet effective joint consists of a protruding tongue on one edge of the workpiece and a corresponding groove on the adjacent edge. When fitted together, the tongue slides snugly into the groove, creating a tight, interlocking connection that prevents movement and ensures a flush surface. Tongue and groove joints are often employed in the construction of cabinets, doors, wainscoting, and hardwood flooring, where precision and stability are paramount.

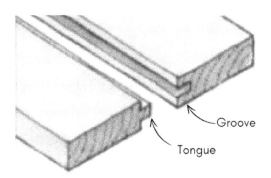

Half-Lap Joints

Half-lap joints are versatile and widely used in millwork construction for joining two pieces of wood at right angles. This joint involves removing half the thickness of each workpiece along their adjoining edges, creating a flush, interlocking connection when fitted together. Half-lap joints are prized for their simplicity, strength, and aesthetic appeal, making them suitable for a variety of applications.

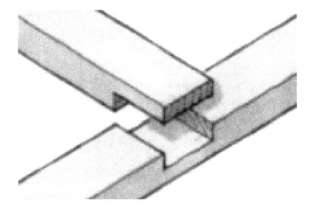

Box Joint (Finger Joint)

Box joints, also known as finger joints, are characterized by interlocking fingers that mesh together to form a sturdy and visually appealing connection. This joint is commonly used in box construction, such as drawers and chests, where strength and durability are paramount. Box joints are cut using specialized jigs or machinery, allowing for precise and repeatable results that showcase the craftsmanship and attention to detail of the millworker.

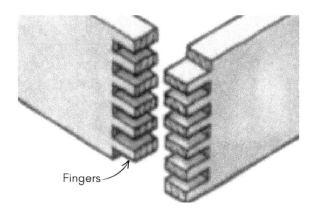

Fingers

Traditional millwork joinery represents the pinnacle of woodworking craftsmanship, blending time-honored techniques with modern innovation to create enduring works of art. Whether it's the intricate dovetails of a handcrafted drawer or the sturdy mortise and tenon joints of a finely crafted cabinet, each example of traditional joinery serves as a testament to the skill, dedication, and ingenuity of the craftsmen who have mastered this timeless craft.

Modern CNC Machining

In the world of millwork, where precision and craftsmanship meet innovation, the advent of Computer Numerical Control (CNC) machining has sparked a transformative revolution. Traditional methods of woodworking have long relied on manual labor and skillful hands to shape raw materials into intricate designs. However, the introduction of CNC technology has elevated millwork to new heights, offering unparalleled precision, efficiency, and versatility.

CNC machining involves the use of computer-controlled machines to precisely cut, carve, and shape various materials, including wood, plastics, metals, and composites. In the millwork industry, CNC routers have become indispensable tools, allowing craftsmen to translate complex designs into flawless creations with remarkable speed and accuracy.

One of the most significant advantages of CNC machining in millwork is its ability to reproduce designs with consistency. Unlike traditional methods, which are susceptible to human error and variability, CNC routers execute tasks with pinpoint precision, ensuring that each component matches the original design specifications perfectly. This level of consistency is invaluable in large-scale production projects, where uniformity is paramount.

Moreover, CNC machining has democratized access to high-quality millwork by streamlining the production process and reducing lead times. Complex designs that once required hours of meticulous manual labor can now be completed in a fraction of the time with CNC technology. This efficiency not only accelerates project timelines but also enables millwork companies to take on a greater volume of work without compromising quality.

Another compelling benefit of CNC machining is its versatility in handling a wide range of materials and design complexities. Whether it's intricate carvings, ornate moldings, or precisely cut panels, CNC routers can tackle virtually any task with ease. This flexibility empowers millwork artisans to push the boundaries of creativity, exploring innovative designs that were previously unattainable through traditional methods.
Furthermore, CNC technology has revolutionized the customization capabilities of millwork. With computer-aided design (CAD) software, designers can create highly detailed and intricate patterns, which CNC routers can execute with unmatched accuracy. This level of customization allows architects, interior designers, and homeowners to bring their visions to life with custom-built millwork solutions tailored to their specific requirements.

In addition to enhancing design possibilities, CNC machining also promotes sustainability in the millwork industry. By optimizing material usage and minimizing waste, CNC routers contribute to eco-friendly manufacturing practices. Furthermore, the precise cutting capabilities of CNC machines reduce the need for rework, conserving resources and minimizing environmental impact.

Despite its numerous advantages, the adoption of CNC machining in the millwork industry has not come without challenges. The initial investment in CNC equipment and training can be significant, requiring millwork companies to carefully weigh the costs against the long-term benefits. Moreover, while CNC technology excels at repetitive tasks and mass production, some purists argue that it lacks the soul and artistry of traditional craftsmanship.

However, as technology continues to advance and CNC machining becomes more accessible and affordable, its role in the millwork industry is poised to expand further. With ongoing innovations in automation, robotics, and artificial intelligence, the future of millwork promises to be even more dynamic and exciting, blending the precision of CNC machining with the timeless beauty of artisanal craftsmanship.

Modern CNC machining has revolutionized the millwork industry, offering unprecedented precision, efficiency, and versatility. From intricate carvings to custom-designed components, CNC routers have empowered millwork artisans to push the boundaries of creativity while streamlining production processes and reducing lead times. As technology continues to evolve, the marriage of CNC machining and traditional craftsmanship holds boundless potential for the future of millwork.

PREFABRICATION AND MODULAR CONSTRUCTION

As a seasoned professional in the millwork industry, I've witnessed firsthand the transformative power of prefabrication and modular construction. These innovative approaches have reshaped the way we design, fabricate, and install millwork components, offering numerous benefits that are impossible to ignore. In this chapter, I'll delve into why prefabrication and modular construction are essential elements of modern millwork practices.

First and foremost, prefabrication and modular construction offer unparalleled efficiency and cost-effectiveness. By manufacturing millwork components off-site in a controlled environment, we can optimize production processes, minimize material waste, and reduce labor costs. This streamlined approach not only accelerates project timelines but also ensures consistency and quality across all components, regardless of the project's scale.

Moreover, prefabrication and modular construction enable greater flexibility and customization in millwork projects. With the ability to prefabricate components according to precise specifications, we can accommodate unique design requirements and tailor solutions to meet the needs of each client. Whether it's a bespoke cabinetry system, intricate architectural paneling, or modular furniture pieces, prefabrication empowers us to bring our clients' visions to life with precision and efficiency.

Another compelling advantage of prefabrication and modular construction is enhanced sustainability. By optimizing material usage and minimizing waste during the manufacturing process, we can reduce our environmental footprint and contribute to eco-friendly building practices. Additionally, the modular nature of prefabricated components allows for easy disassembly, reuse, and recycling, further extending their lifespan and minimizing construction waste.

Furthermore, prefabrication and modular construction offer significant logistical benefits, particularly in challenging or constrained environments. By prefabricating millwork components off-site, we can mitigate the impact of inclement weather, site constraints, and other logistical challenges that may arise during on-site construction. This not only improves project scheduling and coordination but also enhances overall safety and efficiency on the job site.

Incorporating prefabrication and modular construction into our millwork projects also fosters innovation and collaboration within the industry. By leveraging advanced technologies such as Computer-Aided Design (CAD), Computer Numerical Control (CNC) machining, and Building Information Modeling (BIM), we can streamline design processes, improve accuracy, and explore new possibilities in form and function. Moreover, prefabrication encourages collaboration between architects, designers, engineers, and millwork specialists, fostering a multidisciplinary approach to problem-solving and creativity.

Despite these numerous advantages, embracing prefabrication and modular construction in the millwork industry is not without its challenges. Adopting new technologies and methodologies requires investment in training, equipment, and infrastructure, which can be daunting for some businesses. Moreover, there may be resistance to change within traditional sectors of the industry, where manual craftsmanship has long been the norm.

However, the benefits of prefabrication and modular construction far outweigh these challenges, offering a more efficient, sustainable, and innovative approach to millwork design and fabrication. As a passionate advocate for excellence in millwork, I believe that embracing prefabrication and modular construction is essential for staying competitive in today's rapidly evolving construction landscape. By leveraging these innovative approaches, we can elevate the quality of our work, enhance client satisfaction, and pave the way for a brighter future in the millwork industry.

HYBRID MILLWORK CONSTRUCTION METHODS

I've always been fascinated by the intersection of tradition and innovation. While traditional woodworking techniques have stood the test of time, the emergence of modern technologies has opened up new possibilities for creativity, efficiency, and sustainability. In this chapter, I'll share my insights into hybrid millwork construction methods, which seamlessly blend traditional craftsmanship with cutting-edge technologies to deliver exceptional results.

Hybrid millwork construction methods represent a marriage of old-world artistry and contemporary engineering. At their core, these methods embrace the timeless principles of craftsmanship, such as attention to detail, precision, and quality. However, they also harness the power of modern tools and techniques, such as Computer Numerical Control (CNC) machining, digital modeling, and prefabrication, to enhance efficiency and expand design possibilities.

One of the key benefits of hybrid millwork construction methods is their ability to combine the best of both worlds. Traditional woodworking techniques, such as hand carving, joinery, and finishing, imbue millwork pieces with a sense of warmth, character, and authenticity. Meanwhile, modern technologies enable us to achieve levels of precision and consistency that would have been unthinkable using purely manual methods.

For example, imagine crafting a custom-built staircase with intricate balusters and hand-carved details. While traditional craftsmanship may be employed to create the ornate elements by hand, CNC machining can be utilized to fabricate the structural components with unparalleled accuracy. This hybrid approach not only preserves the artisanal quality of the piece but also ensures that it meets the exacting standards of modern construction.

To take it a step further, hybrid millwork construction methods offer significant advantages in terms of efficiency and scalability. By integrating prefabrication and modular construction techniques, we can streamline production processes, minimize waste, and reduce labor costs. This allows us to tackle large-scale projects with greater speed and precision, without sacrificing attention to detail that defines quality millwork.

Another compelling aspect of hybrid millwork construction methods is their potential for innovation and customization. With digital modeling and parametric design software, we can explore virtually limitless design possibilities, pushing the boundaries of form, function, and aesthetics. Whether it's creating complex geometries, experimenting with new materials, or incorporating interactive elements, hybrid methods empower us to help bring our client's vision to reality with unparalleled creativity and precision.

Furthermore, hybrid millwork construction methods align with the growing demand for sustainability and environmental responsibility in the construction industry. By optimizing material usage, minimizing waste, and embracing eco-friendly practices, we can reduce our environmental footprint while delivering high-quality, long-lasting millwork solutions. This commitment to sustainability not only benefits the planet but also enhances our reputation as conscientious professionals in the industry.

Hybrid millwork construction methods represent a harmonious blend of tradition and innovation, offering a holistic approach to craftsmanship in the modern era. By leveraging the best of both worlds, we can achieve superior results that combine the timeless beauty of traditional woodworking with the efficiency, precision, and sustainability of modern technologies. As we continue to explore new techniques and push the boundaries of creativity, hybrid methods will undoubtedly play a central role in shaping the future of the millwork industry.

Tip:

LISP ROUTINES

When it comes to efficiency, automation is pivotal. Using lisp routines is a great way to consolidate mundane and routine tasks to help speed up your draft time and increase your accuracy.

As I started to use AutoCAD day in and day out, I found that sometimes I would run commands or set system or drawing variables many times throughout the day. Let's take a look at some of these commands/variables, and then we will discuss how to automate running them any time you open a drawing with a LISP routine.

The list below explains some of these commands and system variables in detail that are used to write LISP routines.

VTENABLE Command: Transitioning Between AutoCAD views

VTENABLE is a system variable that makes AutoCAD transition between views smoothly or abruptly. The variable can be set to a value of 0-7; I recommend you set it to 1. Setting the variable to 1 will allow you to zoom/pan and "see" where you're zooming from/to. Although this is a system variable, and should only need to be set once, I have found that sometimes the variable can switch to zero when you exit or crash.

PEDITACCEPT Command: Polyline Edits

When running the PEDIT command (Polyline Edit), and you select a line or an arc, AutoCAD will prompt you to turn the object into a polyline.

In most cases you want to turn the object into a polyline anyway, and the prompt is an "extra step." Setting the system variable PEDITACCEPT to 1 will bypass the prompt and turn the object into a polyline automatically.

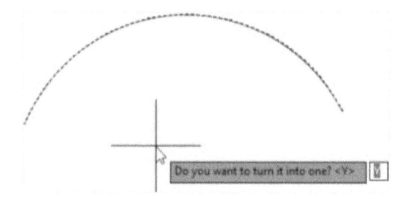

PROXYGRAPHICS

The PROXYGRAPHICS drawing variable is used to tell the drawing to save images of proxy objects (e.g., Civil 3D objects, Architecture toolset objects, etc.). It is also used with those products for specific functionality. In most cases you want this variable to be set to 1, and since it is a drawing variable, you will need to set this to 1 for every drawing.

MSLTSCALE Command: Change Linetypes Variables

Standing for both Model Space LTSCALE and Paper Space LTSCALE, these are drawing variables.

The MSLTSCALE variable controls the linetype display when in model space. When you change the annotation scale, with MSLTSCALE set to 1, your linetypes will scale with the annotation scale. Set to 0, they will show at 1:1. I recommend setting this variable to 1.

FILEDIA Command: File Operations

The infamous FILEDIA variable can be the source of daily migraines. This variable sometimes gets set to 0, causing you to get prompted to actually type in the location for any file operation (e.g., Open, Save As, etc.).

Once you realize that you simply need to set FILEDIA to 1, you want this variable to be set automatically, every time you open AutoCAD………. which leads us to the next section, "How do you setup a startup LISP routine that will run every time you open AutoCAD?"

How to Create a Startup LISP Routine

Creating a startup LISP routine couldn't be easier. Simply create a new text file in a location that you will not change. Then, to get these commands to run, you simply use the LISP function "command" like so:

```
(command "<VARIABLE_NAME>" "<SETTING>")
```

Below is how you would type in all the variables outlined in this article:

```
(command "VTENABLE" "1")
(command "PEDITACCEPT" "1")
(command "PROXYGRAPHICS" "1")
(command "MSLTSCALE" "1")
(command "FILEDIA" "1")
```

Now, save the file and move onto the next step.

Loading Your LISP Routine With Every Drawing

To have your startup LISP file load every time a drawing is open is also very simple. All you have to do is type CUI in the command line. Next, find the LISP Files category in the Customization in All Files section of the CUI dialog box, right-click on it, and choose Load Lisp from the context menu. (*See IMG1*)

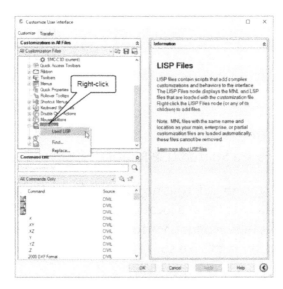

IMG1

Navigate to the location of where your LISP file is, and it will appear in the list. (*See IMG2*)

66

IMG2

And that's how you write and load a startup LISP routine. Remember, if you find other variables or commands that you would like to run every time you open a drawing, simply add them to the startup .LSP file.

4 Dimensioning

THE ROLE OF SHOP DRAWING DIMENSIONS

In the intricate world of architectural millwork, shop drawing dimensions are the roadmap that transforms design concepts into tangible masterpieces. As we embark on this journey, we delve into the precision and craftsmanship that define our profession.

This chapter explores the critical role dimensions play in the fabrication and installation of millwork components. From understanding the importance of clear and accurate dimensions to mastering the translation of design intent into practical measurements, we will equip ourselves with the knowledge and skills necessary to navigate this essential aspect of our craft.

Through practical examples and real-world scenarios, we will learn how to apply shop drawing dimensions effectively, ensuring every detail is meticulously executed to meet the highest standards of quality and precision. From selecting the appropriate dimensioning tools to interpreting complex dimension lines, we will uncover strategies and techniques that streamline the dimensioning process and enhance the clarity and readability of our shop drawings.

Moreover, we will explore the collaborative nature of dimension application, emphasizing the importance of communication and coordination among all those involved in the project. By fostering a culture of collaboration and transparency, we can ensure that shop drawing dimensions accurately reflect the collective vision and goals of the entire project team.

Shop drawing dimensions are like our trusty map, guiding us from design dreams to real-life marvels. As we dive deeper, we find ourselves in what makes our craft so special: precision and artistry.

But it's not just about us; it's about teamwork. Effective communication and coordination among everyone involved in a project are key to getting those dimensions just right. When we all work together, our shop drawing dimensions will truly reflect our shared vision and goals.

Key Components of Dimensions

A more challenging aspect of millwork drafting is dimensioning drawings. While creating dimension objects is fairly straightforward, controlling their appearance and behavior can be difficult. This complexity arises from the numerous types of dimension objects and the various factors that influence their behavior and appearance.

In CAD, there are multiple types of dimension objects available. Common dimensions include linear, radial, diameter, and angular. However, depending on your discipline and/or client, you may need to design other types of dimensions as well. Dimensions in CAD can be added to either the layout space or the model space. In the millwork industry, the decision on where to place dimensions can be contentious. The key factor is ensuring consistency across all drawings for any given project, regardless of how dimensioning is handled. The client's standards should clearly define procedures for handling and positioning dimensions.

A typical dimension has four main components: extension line, dimension line, arrowhead, and dimension text. Each of these can be expressed in various styles, which we will discuss further later. Different disciplines and clients have their own methods for drawing dimensions. To accommodate this, CAD provides a way to customize the appearance of dimensions, called the dimension style.

CAD offers different types of dimensioning, each with its own name:

Manual dimensioning: You draw all the parts of the dimension yourself.

Semiautomatic dimensioning: You specify where the two extension lines go and the location of the dimension line; CAD draws the dimension.

Automatic dimensioning: You select an object, and CAD automatically adds the dimension.

Non-associative dimensioning: Once drawn, the dimension is independent of the object it measures.

True associative dimensioning: The dimension automatically updates when the object is stretched or condensed.
For best practice use, I recommend selecting semiautomatic or true associative dimensions.

To understand the necessity of dimension styles, let's explore their complexity. Each dimension typically consists of four elements:

- Dimension line
- Extension line

- Arrowhead
- Dimension text

Each part has many variables. For example, the arrowhead can be an arrow, a dot, a slash, or nothing at all. The size, color, and layer of the arrowhead can also differ from other dimension elements.

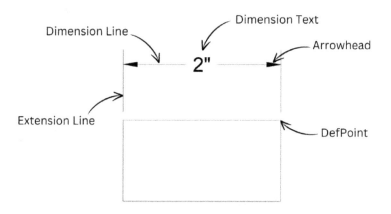

There are four basic types of dimensions:

- Linear dimension
- Aligned dimension
- Radial dimension
- Leader

Other dimension types include baseline, continued, data tables, match lines, callouts, break lines, labeling coordinates, tolerances, coordinate systems, and clearances.

Dimension Standards

Most CAD systems come with presets for several international dimensioning standards. The most common are:

ANSI (American National Standards Institute): Often the default for millwork drawings using imperial units.

DIN (Deutsche Industrie Norm): Defines dimensioning standards for German drawings.

JIS (Japanese Industrial Standard): Defines dimension standards for Japanese drawings.

ISO (International Organization for Standardization): Defines dimension standards for metric drawings.

Geometric tolerancing is a type of dimensioning that specifies how surfaces should be machined.
The following table lists the CAD system variables that differ depending on the selected dimension standard.

Dimension Variable	ANSI	DIN	JIS	ISO
Arrow size	0.1800	2.5000	2.5000	2.5000
Center mark size	0.0900	2.500	0.0000	2.500
Dimension line spacing	0.3800	3.7500	7.0000	3.7500
Extension above dimension line	0.1800	1.2500	1.0000	1.2500
Extension line origin offset	0.0625	0.0625	1.0000	0.0625
Gap from dimension line to text	0.0900	0.6250	0.0000	0.6250
Suppress outside dimension lines	Off	Off	On	Off
Force line inside extension lines	Off	On	On	On
Linear unit format	Decimal	Windows	Decimal	Windows
Alternate units	Decimal	Windows	Decimal	Windows
Scale factor, alternate units	25.4000	0.0394	0.0394	0.0394
Decimal separator	.	.	.	.
Decimal places, alternate units	2	2	2	4
Decimal places, alternate tolerance	2	2	2	4
Place text above the dimension line	Centered	Above	Above	Above
Text inside extensions is horizontal	On	Off	Off	Off
Text outside horizontal	On	Off	Off	Off
Text height	0.1800	2.5000	2.5000	2.5000
Zero suppression	All zeros	Trailing zeros	Trailing zeros	Trailing zeros

Note: You can alter text, move or rotate dimension text, and create oblique extension lines with the DIMEDIT command.

THE IMPORTANCE OF "Verify In Field"

After many years, I've seen my share of shop drawings, where precision is key, and clarity is king. Among the arsenal of tools at our disposal, one principle stands out as a cornerstone of excellence: "Verify In Field" (VIF) dimensioning. Let me explain VIF dimensioning and why it's paramount in the world of millwork shop drawings.

At its core, VIF dimensioning is a proactive approach to ensuring accuracy and alignment between design intent and on-site reality. Unlike traditional drafting methods that rely solely on theoretical measurements, VIF dimensioning empowers us to validate critical dimensions directly in the field, where the millwork will be installed.

Picture a meticulously crafted shop drawing, brimming with precise measurements and intricate details. Yet, despite our best efforts, discrepancies may arise during installation due to site conditions or unforeseen obstacles. This is where VIF dimensioning shines. By embedding a "Verify In Field" directive within our drawings, we anticipate these challenges and provide a mechanism for validation on-site.

But how does VIF dimensioning work in practice? Let me walk you through the process. As we finalize the shop drawings, we identify key dimensions that are critical to the integrity of the millwork installation. These dimensions are tagged with a "VIF" annotation, signaling to installers that verification in the field is necessary to ensure proper fit and alignment.

Once on-site, installers reference the shop drawings and focus their attention on the designated VIF dimensions. Using precision instruments and meticulous attention to detail, they verify that the specified measurements align with the actual conditions within the space. If discrepancies are discovered, they can communicate with the drafting team to adjust the drawings accordingly, ensuring a seamless installation process.

The beauty of VIF dimensioning lies in its ability to bridge the gap between design intent and real-world implementation. By validating critical dimensions in the field, we mitigate the risk of costly errors and delays, fostering a collaborative environment where communication flows freely between the drafting team and on-site personnel.

Moreover, VIF dimensioning promotes a culture of accountability and excellence. It encourages installers to take ownership of the installation process, empowering them to identify and address potential issues proactively. In doing so, we elevate the standard of craftsmanship and uphold the reputation of our industry as purveyors of precision and quality.

As a result, "Verify In Field" dimensioning is more than just a technique—it's a philosophy. It embodies our commitment to excellence and our dedication to delivering millwork of the highest caliber. By integrating VIF dimensioning into our shop drawings, we not only ensure the success of each project but also reaffirm our role as stewards of craftsmanship in an ever-evolving industry.

UNDERSTANDING AWI DIMENSION STANDARDS

The Architectural Woodwork Institute (AWI) is a leading authority in the woodworking industry, providing guidelines and standards to ensure quality, consistency, and excellence in architectural woodwork. Among its many contributions, the AWI Dimension Standards play a crucial role in defining the precise measurements and tolerances for various woodwork elements. Understanding these standards is essential for architects, builders, and woodworkers to achieve optimal results in their projects.

What Are AWI Dimension Standards?

AWI Dimension Standards are a set of guidelines that specify the acceptable dimensions and tolerances for different types of woodwork used in architectural applications. These standards cover a wide range of woodwork elements, including cabinetry, paneling, doors, moldings, and more. They are designed to ensure that woodwork components fit together seamlessly, function correctly, and meet aesthetic and structural requirements.

Key Components of AWI Dimension Standards

1. **Tolerance Levels**

Tolerance levels refer to the permissible variations in dimensions. AWI Dimension Standards outline specific tolerance levels for different types of woodwork. These tolerances ensure that even if there are minor deviations in measurements, the woodwork will still perform its intended function and maintain its visual appeal. For instance, a door panel might have a tolerance level of ±1/16 inch, meaning its dimensions can vary by up to 1/16 inch from the specified measurement without compromising quality.

2. Measurement Units
AWI Dimension Standards use both imperial and metric units, reflecting the global nature of the woodworking industry. It's crucial for professionals to be comfortable working with both measurement systems and to understand how to convert between them accurately. This flexibility helps with catering to diverse markets and clients who may have different preferences.

3. Standard Sizes
Standard sizes for various woodwork components are specified in the AWI Dimension Standards. These sizes are based on common industry practices and are intended to streamline production and installation processes. For example, cabinetry might have standard widths of 12, 15, 18, 24, 30, and 36 inches, making it easier for manufacturers to produce and for installers to fit the pieces together.

4. Material Specifications
The standards also include guidelines for the types of materials that should be used for different applications. This includes the species of wood, the grade, and the finish. Material specifications ensure that the woodwork not only meets aesthetic standards but also performs well under various environmental conditions.

Benefits of Adhering to AWI Dimension Standards

1. Quality Assurance
By following AWI Dimension Standards, woodworkers can ensure that their products meet high-quality benchmarks. This adherence minimizes the risk of errors, rework, and customer dissatisfaction.

2. Consistency
Standardized dimensions and tolerances help achieve consistency across different projects and components. This consistency is vital for large-scale projects where multiple elements must fit together seamlessly.

3. Efficiency
Knowing the standard dimensions and tolerances allows for more efficient planning, production, and installation. It reduces the need for custom adjustments and modifications, saving time and resources.

4. Professional Credibility
Adhering to recognized standards like those from AWI enhances the credibility and reputation of woodworking professionals. It demonstrates a commitment to excellence and a thorough understanding of industry's best practices.

Challenges and Considerations

While AWI Dimension Standards provide numerous benefits, there are also challenges and considerations to keep in mind:

1. Adapting to Custom Projects

Not all projects will fit within the standard dimensions and tolerances. Custom projects may require deviations from the standards, necessitating careful planning and communication with clients.

2. Material Variability

Natural wood can have inherent variability, including knots, grain patterns, and color differences. Professionals must account for these factors while adhering to dimensional standards.

3. Training and Education

Staying up to date with AWI Dimension Standards requires ongoing training and education. Woodworkers need to be familiar with the latest guidelines and how to apply them effectively.

AWI Dimension Standards are a cornerstone of quality and consistency in the woodworking industry. By understanding and adhering to these standards, professionals can ensure their work meets the highest criteria for precision, functionality, and aesthetics. Whether for standard or custom projects, these guidelines provide a foundation for excellence that benefits manufacturers, installers, and clients alike.

Tip:

USING TOOL PALETTES

Tool palettes provide me with instant access to a complete inventory of AutoCAD tools—such as cabinets, shortcuts, and hardware—all within one consistent user interface. They're highly visual, offering previews of styles, and I have the ability to create custom tool palettes tailored to my specific design needs. For instance, I can craft a palette to house a list of commonly used symbols, commands, and blocks.

Tool palettes groups are part of the tool palettes set and contain collections of tools, each representing individual tabs. The AutoCAD toolset provides several tool palettes from the Sample Palette catalog, but I can also create new ones within the toolset or in the Content Browser.

Within the tool palettes sets, which contain groups of tool palettes, I have the flexibility to rename the default set or create a custom one. I can also add, remove, and rearrange palettes and groups within the set.

There are several methods to build your own custom tool palettes.

Here's an example of dragging or clicking and placing a callout bubble from the Annotation tab"

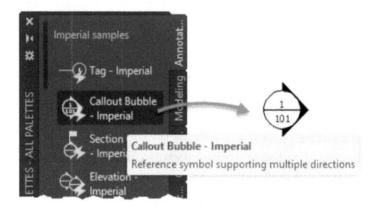

Methods for Creating Tool Palettes

You can easily create a new tool palette:

- Use the tool palette shortcut menu to create a new, empty palette.

- Use a Design Center shortcut menu to create a tool palette tab with selected content.

Tool Palette Content

Tool palettes can contain a variety of types of tools. These tools are ideal for adding objects such as the following:

- Blocks
- Hatches and fills
- Tables

Other types of supported content include geometric objects, dimensions, xrefs, and raster images. You can also add lights, cameras, visual styles, and materials (not available in AutoCAD LT).

Methods for Adding Tools to Tool Palettes

You can add tools to a new or existing tool palette using several methods:

- Drag objects from your drawing onto the palette.
- Drag drawings, blocks, and hatches from the Design Center. Drawings that are added to a tool palette are inserted as blocks when dragged into the drawing.
- Drag toolbar buttons from the Customize dialog box.
- Drag commands from the Command List pane on the Customize User Interface (CUI) Editor.
- Paste tools from one tool palette to another.

Customize Tool Palettes

Once you've created a palette, you can modify it to suit your needs.
Several options are available from shortcut menus:

- Rearrange the tools on a palette with a sort option. You can also drag tools directly onto the palette.
- Add text and separator lines.
- Move a tool palette tab up and down the list of tabs by using the shortcut menu or the Customize dialog box.
- Delete any tool palettes that you no longer need.
- Set the path to your tool palettes on the Files tab in

the Options dialog box. This path can be to a shared network location.

- Associate a customizable tool palette group with each panel on the ribbon.
- Change the palette's read-only status in the Palettes folder. If a tool palette is set to be read-only, a lock icon is displayed in a lower corner of the tool palette. This indicates that you cannot modify the tool palette beyond changing its display settings and rearranging the icons.

Palette Groups

To organize and reduce the number of tool palettes in the tool palettes window, you can define and display tool palette groups. A tool palette group limits the number of palettes displayed in the Tool Palettes window. The Customize Palettes option provides options to create and organize tool palette groups.

In the example below, you can drag a palette from the list in the left pane under a group in the right pane.

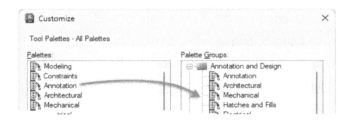

5 Shaping Tomorrow

In the world of architecture and interior design, millwork has long been a cornerstone, contributing to the aesthetic and functional aspects of spaces. From custom cabinetry to intricate moldings, millwork involves the fine craftsmanship of wood, and other materials to create components that enhance the beauty and utility of buildings. However, as we move into the future, millwork is not just about tradition— it's about innovation, sustainability, and the integration of cutting-edge technology. Here's how I see millwork shaping tomorrow's future.

Sustainability at the Forefront

One of the most significant trends in millwork is the shift towards sustainable practices. As environmental concerns become more pressing, the demand for eco-friendly materials and processes in construction and design is growing. Millwork is leading the way by embracing sustainable sourcing, using reclaimed or responsibly harvested wood, and incorporating recycled materials.

Additionally, the industry is adopting low-VOC (volatile organic compound) finishes and adhesives, reducing the environmental impact and improving indoor air quality. This focus on sustainability not only helps in preserving natural resources but also aligns with the growing consumer demand for green building practices.

This is where LEED (Leadership in Energy and Environmental Design) comes into the picture. The growing availability of sustainable materials and technologies is making it easier and more cost-effective for companies to meet LEED standards. As the industry continues to evolve, those who embrace LEED and other green building certifications will likely find themselves at the forefront of innovation and industry leadership.

LEED is more than just a certification; it's a commitment to a more sustainable future. In the millwork industry, where the use of natural resources is integral to the craft, LEED provides a clear path to environmental responsibility, operational efficiency, and market competitiveness. As sustainability continues to shape the future of construction and design, millwork companies that prioritize LEED will not only contribute to a healthier planet but will also secure their place in an increasingly green marketplace.

By embracing LEED, the millwork industry can achieve a balance between tradition and innovation, craftsmanship and sustainability—ensuring that the beauty of woodwork is matched by a commitment to preserving the natural world for future generations.

Technology Integration: Precision and Efficiency

The integration of technology in millwork is transforming the industry, making it more efficient and precise than ever before. Computer Numerical Control (CNC) machines, 3D modeling software, and laser cutting technologies are now standard in modern millwork shops. These tools allow for the creation of highly intricate designs that would be difficult or impossible to achieve by hand.

Moreover, the use of Building Information Modeling (BIM) allows millwork designs to be fully integrated into the broader construction process, ensuring that all elements fit perfectly with the overall building plans. This not only reduces waste but also minimizes errors and ensures that projects are completed faster and more accurately.

Customization and Personalization

Today's consumers are increasingly looking for unique, personalized spaces that reflect their tastes and lifestyles. Millwork is perfectly positioned to meet this demand. With advanced design software and precision machinery, millworkers can create custom pieces that are tailored to the specific needs and preferences of clients. Whether it's a custom-built bookshelf that fits perfectly into a quirky corner or a kitchen island designed to optimize workflow, millwork allows for a level of customization that mass-produced furniture simply cannot match.

Furthermore, the use of digital tools enables designers and clients to collaborate more effectively, visualizing and tweaking designs before any wood is cut. This collaborative process ensures that the final product meets expectations and adds a personal touch to the space.

Smart Spaces and Millwork

As smart technology becomes more integrated into our daily lives, millwork is evolving to accommodate and enhance these innovations. Custom cabinetry and furniture are being designed with built-in smart features, such as charging stations, hidden compartments for electronics, and integrated lighting. This seamless integration of technology and millwork not only improves the functionality within the space but also keeps them looking clean and uncluttered.

Moreover, millwork is playing a crucial role in the design of smart homes and offices, where the focus is on creating environments that are not only aesthetically pleasing but also responsive to the needs of the occupants. This could involve everything from hidden panels that conceal entertainment systems to custom desks with ergonomic features tailored to the user.

The Future of Millwork: Innovation Meets Tradition

While millwork is steeped in tradition, its future lies in innovation. The industry is poised to continue evolving, driven by advancements in technology, sustainability, and a growing desire for personalized, functional spaces. As we look to the future, millwork will play a crucial role in shaping the environments we live and work in, combining the craftsmanship of the past with the possibilities of tomorrow.

Whether it's creating sustainable, eco-friendly spaces, integrating smart technology, or crafting custom pieces that reflect individual style, millwork is at the forefront of the design and construction industries. Its ability to adapt and innovate ensures that it will remain a vital component of our built environment for years to come.

As millwork continues to evolve, it will shape the future of architecture and interior design, blending tradition with modern innovation to create spaces that are not only beautiful but also sustainable, efficient, and personalized. The future of millwork is bright, and it's exciting to imagine the possibilities that lie ahead.

AI-TOCAD

In the realm of design and engineering, AutoCAD stands as a cornerstone, revolutionizing the way professionals create, visualize, and document their ideas. As we stand on the cusp of technological advancement, the integration of Artificial Intelligence (AI) into AutoCAD promises to redefine the landscape of design, offering efficiency, precision, and innovation like never before.

The Evolution of AutoCAD

AutoCAD, developed by Autodesk in 1982, quickly became the standard software for Computer-Aided Design (CAD). Its intuitive interface and powerful tools enabled architects, engineers, and designers to transform concepts into tangible designs with unprecedented ease and accuracy.

Over the years, AutoCAD has evolved significantly, incorporating 3D modeling, cloud collaboration, and mobile capabilities, among other features. Each iteration has aimed to streamline workflows and enhance productivity, reflecting the ever-changing needs of the design industry.

Enter Artificial Intelligence

The integration of AI into AutoCAD marks the dawn of a new era in design technology. AI brings with it a myriad of capabilities that augment the traditional functionalities of AutoCAD, propelling it into realms previously unexplored.

1. **Design Optimization**:

AI algorithms can analyze vast datasets and user preferences to generate design options optimized for various criteria such as cost, sustainability, and functionality. By leveraging machine learning, AutoCAD mixed with AI can iteratively refine designs based on feedback, ultimately delivering solutions that surpass human intuition alone.

2. **Generative Design**:

Generative design, empowered by AI, allows designers to define parameters and constraints before letting algorithms explore countless design permutations. AutoCAD, when infused with AI, becomes a creative partner, producing innovative solutions that push the boundaries of conventional design thinking.

3. **Automated Drafting**:

Gone are the days of manual drafting. With AI, AutoCAD can automate repetitive tasks such as drawing annotations, dimensioning, and layer management. This automation not only accelerates the design process but also minimizes errors, ensuring precision and consistency across projects.

4. **Intelligent Assistance**:

Imagine having an AI assistant embedded within AutoCAD, capable of providing real-time suggestions, flagging potential errors, and offering contextual guidance as you design – well, it's here. This intelligent assistance fosters a collaborative environment where designers can leverage AI's expertise to enhance their creativity and efficiency.

The Future Landscape

As AI continues to advance, too will the capabilities of AutoCAD. The future holds the promise of seamless integration between AI and design software, blurring the lines between human creativity and machine intelligence.

1. Personalized Workflows:
AutoCAD with AI will adapt to the unique preferences and workflows of individual users, offering personalized recommendations and tools tailored to their specific needs. This customization enhances user experience and empowers designers to work more efficiently.

2. Augmented Reality (AR) Integration:
With the rise of AR technology, future iterations of AutoCAD may incorporate augmented reality features, allowing designers to visualize their creations in the real world. AI algorithms could analyze spatial data and environmental factors, providing insights that inform design decisions in real-time.

3. Ethical and Sustainable Design:
AI-powered AutoCAD will play a pivotal role in promoting ethical and sustainable design practices. By analyzing environmental impact, material efficiency, and lifecycle considerations, AI can assist designers in creating solutions that prioritize sustainability without compromising functionality or aesthetics.

The convergence of AutoCAD and AI heralds a transformative era in design, characterized by unprecedented efficiency, creativity, and sustainability. As technology continues to evolve, too will the capabilities of AutoCAD, empowering designers to push the boundaries of innovation and shape a brighter future for generations to come. Embracing this symbiotic relationship between human ingenuity and artificial intelligence, we embark on a journey towards a world where design knows no bounds.

NAVIGATING MILLWORK DRAFTING ETIQUETTE

As a weathered millwork drafter, I've learned that professionalism and collaboration are essential for success in the industry. Whether you're working independently or as part of a team, adhering to millwork drafting etiquette can foster positive working relationships, streamline communication, and ensure the successful completion of projects. In this chapter, I'll share my insights and tips on navigating millwork drafting etiquette with grace and professionalism.

Clear Communication is Key

One of the fundamental principles of millwork drafting etiquette is clear communication. Whether you're discussing project requirements with a client or collaborating with colleagues, it's essential to communicate clearly, concisely, and respectfully. Be proactive in seeking clarification when needed and provide updates on your progress regularly. By maintaining open lines of communication, you can avoid misunderstandings, minimize errors, and build trust with your team and clients.

Respect Design Intent

As a millwork drafter, it's important to respect the design intent of the project and work closely with architects, designers, and other constituents to bring their vision to life. Take the time to familiarize yourself with the project requirements, design specifications, and aesthetic preferences of the client. Be mindful of any constraints or limitations that may impact the design process and collaborate with the design team to find creative solutions that meet the client's needs while adhering to budget and schedule constraints.

Adhere to Standards and Best Practices

In the world of millwork drafting, consistency and precision are paramount. Adhering to industry standards, best practices, and company protocols is essential for producing high-quality drawings that meet or exceed client expectations. Follow established drafting conventions, such as layer naming conventions, linetypes, and dimensioning standards, to ensure consistency across projects. Additionally, stay abreast of industry trends, emerging technologies, and new drafting techniques to continuously improve your skills and expertise.

Embrace Feedback and Constructive Criticism

Feedback is an invaluable tool for growth and improvement in millwork drafting. Embrace feedback from colleagues, supervisors, and clients as an opportunity to learn, grow, and refine your skills. Be receptive to constructive criticism and take proactive steps to address any areas for improvement. Use feedback as a catalyst for professional development, seeking out opportunities for training, mentorship, and skill enhancement to further your career in millwork drafting.

Practice Professionalism and Integrity

Above all, professionalism and integrity are the cornerstones of millwork drafting etiquette. Treat your colleagues, clients, and collaborators with respect, courtesy, and professionalism at all times. Be honest, transparent, and accountable in your interactions, taking ownership of your work, good or bad, and delivering on your commitments. Uphold ethical standards and avoid conflicts of interest or behaviors that may compromise your integrity or reputation in the industry.

Navigating millwork, drafting etiquette requires a commitment to professionalism, collaboration, and continuous improvement. By communicating clearly, respecting design intent, adhering to standards and best practices, embracing feedback, and practicing professionalism and integrity, you can cultivate positive working relationships, produce high-quality drawings, and contribute to the success of your projects and your career in millwork drafting. Let's strive to uphold the highest standards of etiquette and professionalism in our work, fostering a culture of excellence and integrity in the millwork industry.

Tip:

ORTHOGRAPHIC DRAFTING

I would be remiss if I didn't go over the absolute importance of incorporating orthographic drafting into your toolset. In the realm of technical drawing and design, precision is paramount. Whether you're an architect, engineer, or drafter, the ability to convey complex ideas clearly and accurately is essential. This is where orthogonal drafting in AutoCAD comes into play. Orthogonal, or orthographic, drafting is a fundamental technique that involves creating two-dimensional representations of three-dimensional objects, with each view oriented perpendicularly to the object.

Orthogonal drafting, often referred to as orthographic projection, is a method of drawing where different views of an object (such as the top, front, and side) are projected onto planes that are perpendicular to each other. Each view is a 2D representation of the object as seen from a specific angle, and when combined, these views provide a comprehensive understanding of the object's geometry. This approach is crucial for creating accurate technical drawings that are used in manufacturing, construction, and other industries.

Drafting Orthogonally in AutoCAD provides a number of key attributes:

1. Accuracy and Precision
2. Clarity in Communication
3. Comprehensive Visualization
4. Standardization and Consistency
5. Facilitating Manufacturing and Construction

Best Practices for Orthogonal Drafting in AutoCAD

Enable Ortho Mode: Use Ortho mode (`F8`) to constrain the movement of your cursor to horizontal or vertical directions, ensuring your lines are perfectly aligned.

Use Layers: Organize your drawing by using layers for different views and elements. This helps keep your drawing organized and allows for easy visibility management.

Dimension Accurately: Use AutoCAD's dimensioning tools to provide precise measurements in your drawings. This ensures that your design can be accurately interpreted and executed.

Regularly Check Alignments: Use tools like the `PROJECTGEOMETRY` command or the 'XLINE' command to ensure that features in different views are properly aligned, maintaining consistency across your drawing.

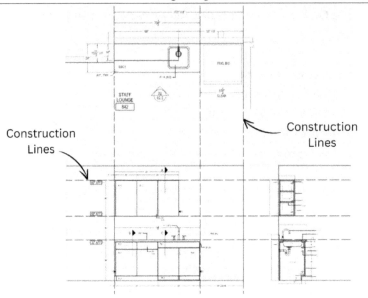

Construction Lines

Construction Lines

Drafting orthogonally in AutoCAD is not just a technical skill but a crucial practice that underpins the accuracy, clarity, and reliability of technical drawings. Whether you're designing a complex machine component or an architectural structure, orthogonal drafting ensures that your designs are both precise and easy to understand. By mastering this technique in AutoCAD, you enhance your ability to communicate design intent clearly and effectively, paving the way for successful project execution and high-quality outcomes.

Orthogonal drafting is the foundation upon which many industries build their designs, making it an indispensable skill for any professional in the field.

GLOSSARY

In the intricate world of millwork, a solid understanding of industry-specific terminology is essential for clear communication and precision in design and manufacturing. This millwork glossary serves as a reference, providing definitions and explanations of the key terms and concepts used in the trade. Whether you're a seasoned professional or new to the field, this glossary will help you navigate some of the language of millwork with confidence and clarity.

A

Access Panel
A removable panel which provides access to space behind.

Adjustable Shelves
Shelves whose location can be adjusted through the use of pins (or brackets) set into line-bored holes or metal clips on a ladder-type shelf standard.

Anchorage Fastener
Installation screws used to attach casework or blocking to walls.

Apron
For purposes of these standards, it means a horizontal trim member that extends vertically below a horizontal surface such as a countertop or table typically at knee spaces or open sink areas.

Architectural Woodwork

Custom wood products including interior woodwork attached to a building (except specialty items such as flooring, shingles, exposed roof decking, ceiling, siding, structural wood trusses and rafters, and overhead type doors). May be composed of wood, laminate, or solid surface materials.

B

Backer Material

A sheet product, applied to the backs of panels, countertops and splashes, with performance properties determined by its material composition. Because material composition types vary, backer sheet types vary in performance properties. The type of backer sheet material used should be based on overall product demands.

Balanced Construction

A term used to describe a panel made up of an odd number of plies laminated together so that the materials are identical on both sides of a plane through the center of the panel. To achieve balanced construction, materials should be used on either side that contract or expand, or are moisture permeable, at the same rate.

Banded, Edgeband

Usually refers to the application of a material to the edge of a panel to cover or hide the otherwise exposed core.

Base

The support assembly between the cabinet's bottom component and the floor.

Baseboard

A board running along the bottom of an interior wall, covering the joint between the wall and the floor.

Base Cabinet

A unit of casework which is supported entirely by the floor and contains an external work surface. The height of a base cabinet, from the finished floor to the countertop surface, ranging from 28" to 38". The depth of a base cabinet, from the front of the cabinet door/drawer to the face of the wall, ranges from 22" to 30".

Bevel, Bevelled Edge

A machined angle other than a right angle or, in flooring or wall paneling, a V-shaped groove between strips, planks, or panels.

Blind Corner

The butting of two cabinets, typically with filler strips, at an approximate 90 degree angle, resulting in an empty space in the back corner.

Bucks

In-wall blocking used for the installation of door/window jambs and other woodwork in conjunction with metal framing and/or block walls.

Bullnose

A convex, rounded shape typically applied to edges of countertops, stair steps, and trim moulding.

Butt Joint

A joint formed by square-edged surfaces (ends, edges, faces) coming together; end butt joint, edge butt joint.

C

Cabinet

A single, manufactured case typically consists of two ends, a top, a bottom, and may include back, stretchers, anchor strips, shelves, doors, drawer fronts, drawers, dividers, and hardware.

Cantilever

A projecting structure that is attached or supported at only one end, such as an extended countertop.

Casework

Base, tall, and wall cabinets, display fixtures, and storage shelving units. The generic term for both "boxes" and special desks, reception counters, nurse's stations, etc. Generally, it includes countertops and work surfaces.

Closure Panel, Filler

A trim component at top of tall cabinets or top and bottom of wall cabinets used to fill the space between a casework unit and the adjacent wall or casework unit.

Concealed Surface

Surfaces that are neither visible nor accessible to the building occupants and/or general public under normal circumstances.

Cope

On profiled moulding, to cut the end of one member to match the profile of another member; often used to form interior corner joints in mouldings.

Core

The panel material on which an exposed surface material (typically veneer or decorative laminate) is applied. Examples include: particleboard, MDF, veneer, lumber, or a combination of these.

Core, Hallow

A core assembly generally used in doors, consisting of a frame assembly with open areas typically filled with an expandable cardboard/paper honeycomb material.

Cup

A deviation in the face of a piece from a straight line drawn from end to end of a piece. It is measured at the point of greatest distance from the straight line.
Note: Cupping occurs when panels (such as doors/drawer fronts) aren't properly balanced.

Custom Grade

One of three aesthetic grades in regard to material and workmanship. Appropriate for the majority of projects. In the absence of specification, this is the default grade to be applied.

D

Dado Joint

A rectangular groove across the grain of a wood member into which the end of the joining member is inserted; also, a housed joint.
Also, mortise-and-tenon and stopped or blind dado.

Die Wall

A woodwork assembly, typically vertical, consisting of sub-framing as the support for countertops and finished faces as well as a chase way for wiring. Often self-supporting or free-standing.
Commonly used for reception desks, nurse stations and low-walls.

Dovetail Joint

A joinery technique consisting of one or more tenons cut to extend from the end of one board and interlock with a corresponding series of mortises cut into the end of another board. When glued, a wooden dovetail joint requires no mechanical fasteners.

E

Eased Edge

The result of a process in which sharp edges are traditionally "eased" by lightly striking the edge with a fine abrasive. May also be machined to a small radius when permitted by specification.

Economy Grade

One of three aesthetic grades in regard to material and workmanship. Appropriate for work where price is a major factor and relaxing of tolerances is acceptable. Typical areas for use include back rooms as well as utility storage areas.

Exposed Interior Surfaces

For the purposes of these standards, specifically casework, generally means all interior surfaces exposed to view in open casework or behind transparent doors (i.e. glass).

F

Face Frame

Components attached to the front of a cabinet body which overlay the edges of the carcass and provide an attachment point for doors and external hardware.

Filler

A trim component used in conjunction with the installation of casework to close or span voids between casework units or interior walls. *Also see Closure Panel.*

Finger Joint

A series of precise, interlocking fingers cut on the ends of two matching pieces of wood that mesh together and are held rigidly in place with adhesive to increase the length of the board or molding.

Flush Inset

Cabinet construction in which the door and drawer faces are set within and flush with the body members or face frames of the cabinet with spaces between face surfaces sufficient for operating clearance.

Flush Overlay

Cabinet construction in which door and drawer faces cover the body members of the cabinet with minimal spaces between face surfaces within the clearances outlined in the standards.

French Cleat

A method of concealed panel or casework installation, consisting of two pieces of solid lumber or panel product, each having one edge machined at an angle. One piece is attached to the wall while the other is attached to the back of the casework product such that the pieces will lock together when the casework is hung.
Often used for wall cabinets and wall panels.

Furring

Material added to a building surface to create a true plane in order to install woodwork plumb and level.

G

GC, General Contractor

A person responsible for executing the contract for a building project and coordinating the work between the subcontractors as well as the chain of communications between the owner, design professionals, and subcontractors.

Grade

A measurable evaluation ranking (i.e. AWI aesthetic grades such as PREMIUM, CUSTOM, or ECONOMY).

Grain

Refers to the visual appearance of lumber and veneer.

H

Hairline

Refers to the visual appearance of lumber and veneer.

Half Lap Joint

A joint formed by extending (lapping) the joining part of one member over the joining part of another. Both members are machined at the joint, removing half the thickness of each member so that when joined all surfaces are flush.

Hardboard

A generic term for a panel manufactured primarily from processed dense fibers and conforming to the requirements of ANSI/AHA A 135.4.

High-Pressure Decorative Laminate (HPDL), Laminate

Laminated thermoset decorative sheets, intended for decorative purposes, consist of phenolic resin-impregnated sheets of fibrous material or paper and a melamine resin-impregnated decorative top layer in various colors and textures. The sheets are bonded under the combined effect of high heat and pressure, thus producing a highly durable product.

I

Integral Ends
End components that are part of a cabinet body. These ends are not added to cover an existing end component and are not removable.

Intermediate Rail
In face frame or door construction, a horizontal component that connects to both stiles between the top and bottom rails.

Internal Blocking
Wooden or metal support material placed within drywall or plaster walls to support casework installations.

J

Joint
The line of juncture between the edges or ends of two adjacent pieces of lumber or sheets of veneer, such as butt, dado (blind, stopped), dovetail, blind dovetail, finger, half-lap, lock, miter (shoulder, lock, spline), mortise-and-tenon (blind slotted, stub, or through), rabbet, scarf, spline, and tongue-and-groove joint.

Joint, Shop

Any joints or a combination of joints and/or mechanical fasteners, that are used to join two woodwork parts in the shop (factory).

Joint, Field

Any joints or a combination of joints and/or mechanical fasteners that are used to join two members in the field.

K

Kerf

The groove or notch made as a saw passes through wood and/or the wood removed by the saw in parting the material.
Commonly used to create curved panels.

Knocked Down, KD

Unassembled, as contrasted to assembled.
Synonymously referred to as modular.

L

Lacquer

A finished coating applied to wood or metal.
Commonly referred to as paint.

Leveller
Adjustable casework support hardware.

Louver
A slat or slats installed in a panel or door at an angle to the panel, allowing various degrees of light, air, or sound passage.

Lumber
Pieces of wood thicker than ¼" manufactured no further than by sawing, planning, crosscutting to length, and perhaps edge machined.

M

Manufacturer
A person or organization that regularly engages in the practice of manufacturing, refinishing, and/or installing architectural woodwork.

Medium Density Fiberboard, MDF
A generic term for a panel manufactured by breaking down hardwood or softwood residuals into wood fibers, often in a defibrator, combining it with wax and a resin binder, and forming panels by applying high temperature and pressure.

Member

An individual piece of solid stock or plywood that forms an item of woodwork.

Miter Joint

The joining of two members at an angle that bisects the angle of junction.

Miterfold

An assembly made from a single panel in one machining process that usually consists of machining two edges at forty-five degree angles; includes placement of tape, machining, application of adhesive, folding, gluing, clamping, and cleanup.

Mock Up

A sample made by the manufacturer to demonstrate materials, assembly, workmanship, finish, and/or tolerances proposed for a project.

Mortise and Tenon

A wood joinery technique where the end of one member is machined to form a rectangular projection (tenon) designed to fit tightly into a corresponding cavity (mortise) in the adjoining member.
There are multiple variations of the joint; blind, slotted, stub and through.

Moulding

A decorative strip of material, usually having a curved or profiled face or edge, though it may also be square.

Mullion

A vertical or horizontal component that creates a division between a window, screen unit, or other opening.

N

Nominal

The average sizes (width and thickness) of lumber just out of the sawmill before processed into a usable board stock. Always larger than the finished dimensions.

Nosing

A round convex edge, as on a stair step.

O

Overlay

To superimpose or laminate a wood veneer or a decorative laminate, such as melamine, polyester, or high-pressure decorative laminate, to one or both sides of a given core, such as plywood, particleboard, or MDF.

P

Particleboard, PBC

A generic term for a panel manufactured from materials in the form of discrete particles, as distinguished from fibers. Other materials may have been added during manufacturing to improve certain properties, including density.

Partition

A panel or assembly of panels that is securely attached to floor, ceiling, walls, or a supported frame used to divide spaces.

Plank

A board, usually lumber, laid with its wide dimension horizontal and used as a bearing surface.

Plinth

A block or base supporting a column, pedestal, or casework.

Plywood, Ply

A panel composed of a crossbanded assembly of layers or plies of veneer that are joined with an adhesive. An odd number of plies is always used.

Premium Grade

One of three aesthetic grades in regard to material and workmanship. Intended for the finest work.
Recommended for high visibility areas in which a design professional or owner wants to make a "statement". The exacting tolerances and stricter guidelines for materials required in premium grade reflect a higher dollar value.

Priming

In finishing, refers to the initial layer of a coating onto which subsequent coats will adhere to.

PVC, PVC Edge

A polyvinyl chloride edgebanding material. Typically, available in seamless rolls and applied using edgebanding machines with hot-melt adhesives.

Q

Quirk

Refers to a kerf in mouldings or a reveal in panels that can hide the use of mechanical fasteners or imperfections.

R

Rabbet

Rectangular cut on the edge of a part; a "rabbet" has two surfaces forming an "L" shape.

Rail

The horizontal components of a stile and rail door assembly or face frame. Also refers to the horizontal components of the core assembly of a wood flushed door or panel.

Raised Panel

A traditional door or wall panel with a bevel-edge captured in a stile and rail frame.

Return

Continuation in a different direction of a moulding or projection, usually at right angles.

Reveal

The space between adjacent panels or other architectural features that allow for panel expansion and contraction.

Reveal Overlay

Cabinet construction method in which the door and drawer faces partially cover the body members or face frames of the cabinet with spaces between face surfaces creating decorative reveals.

Running Trim

Generally combined in the term "standing and running trim" and refers to random length trims delivered to the jobsite (i.e. baseboard, chair rail, crown moulding). Running trim is generally installed horizontally. Standing trim is installed vertically.

S

S4S

An abbreviation of "Surfaced on Four Sides" used to describe dimensional components which have two flat and parallel faces, two flat and parallel edges, and square 90-degree corners. Generally, lumber classified as S4S has the finish size specified.

Scribe

To mark and cut an item of woodwork so that it will fit the irregular contours of an uneven wall, floor, or other adjoining surface.

Self-Edge

The application of material to an edge that matches the face.

Semi-Exposed Surfaces

Surfaces that are generally neither visible nor accessible to the building occupants and/or general public but can be made visible or accessible by the movement of a component.

Shop Drawings

Detailed engineering drawings produced by the manufacturer for the fabrication of architectural woodwork products. Shop drawings are often submitted to design professionals for review and comment.

Solid Surface

Filled cast polymeric resin panel of homogeneous composition. Solid surfaces require polishing but have no applied finish coat and may be capable of being fabricated with inconspicuous seams and restored to its original finish.

Species

A classification used to identify lumber based on characteristics inherent in the tree.

Splash

A vertical countertop component along the back and/or end sides, intended to seal the countertop and protect the adjacent surfaces. A splash can be integral to the counter or secondary applied.

Spline

A thin, narrow strip inserted into matching grooves that have been machined in abutting edges of panels or lumber to ensure a flush alignment and a secure joint.

Stile

The vertical components of a door or window frame, often used in the construction of panels.

Stile and Rail Construction

A method of construction consisting of a panel captured within a frame. Its most basic form consists of five members; the panel and the four members that make up the frame. The vertical members of the frame are called stiles while the horizontal members are known as rails.

Stretcher

Structural casework component that spans between the ends of a cabinet body. Stretchers may be oriented horizontally or vertically.

Substrate

The material to which a veneer or laminate is bonded to create a working surface.

Subtop

The separate panel fastened on the top of cabinets or furniture over which the decorative countertop is placed.

T

Tall Cabinet

A unit of casework that measures more than 72" in height. The height of a tall cabinet, from the finished floor to the cabinet top ranges from 72" up to 96". The depth of tall cabinet, from the front of the cabinet door to the face of the wall ranging from 12" to 30".

Tenon, Tongue

The projecting tongue-like part of a wood member to be inserted into a slot (mortise) of another member to form a mortise and tenon joint.

Toe Kick

The recessed area at the bottom of a base or tall cabinet.

V

V-Grooved

Narrow and shallow V or U-shaped channels machined on the surface edges of wood to achieve a decorative effect.

Veneer

A thin layer of wood, sliced from a log of flitch. Thickness varies from, but not exceed 0.012" to 0.252" thick.

W

Wainscot

A lower interior wall surface that contrasts with the wall surface above it.

Wall Cabinet

A unit of casework which is supported entirely by a wall. The height of wall cabinet, including the light apron ranges from 12" up to 48". The depth of a wall cabinet, from the front of the cabinet door to the face of the wall, ranges from 12" to 16".

ABOUT THE AUTHOR

I had been exposed to CAD in my younger years during the Release 14 days, but didn't take it seriously until I landed my first job at a furniture manufacturing company, it was here I discovered my love for millwork. There was something about the smell of freshly cut wood and the transformation into beautiful furniture that really resonated with me.

It was also at this job that I was reintroduced to CAD, this time through a software you may have never heard of, called Drafix. With the encouragement of supportive coworkers, I gave CAD a second chance, and that's when things begin to click for me.

For over 20 years since, I've had the opportunity to work with various millwork manufacturers all across the US, learning from passionate woodworkers. What I enjoy most is the collaboration, the sense of accomplishment from our efforts, and the challenge of pushing the limits of architectural millwork.